I BROKE THE CURSE

Dr. Jackie Kinslow

I Broke the Curse
Dr. Jackie Kinslow

Copyright © 2021 by Dr. Jackie Kinslow

Cover Art & Formatting 2021 by Traces of Design

Published by TAWCarlisle Publishing, LLC

ISBN 978-1-7367513-2-9

All Scripture quotations, unless otherwise indicated, are taken from THE HOLY BIBLE, KNG JAMES VERSION ®, KJV® Copyright © 1973, 1978, 1984, 2011 by Biblica, Inc.™ Used by permission. All rights are reserved worldwide.

Verses marked NIV are taken from New International Version Copyright © 1973, 1978, 1984 by International Bible Society. All rights are reserved.

All rights reserved. The reproduction, transmission, or utilization of this work in whole in any form by any electronic, mechanical or other means, now known or hereafter invented, including xerography, photocopying, and recording, or in any information storage or retrieval system, is forbidden without written permission.
For permission, please contact TAWCarlisle Publishing, 1402 21st Street, Sacramento, CA 95811 Attn: Permissions.

Printed in the United States of America

DEDICATION

In memory and in honor of my husband, the late Suffragan Bishop Arthur Gene Kinslow. I dedicate my book to you, the love of my life for thirty-nine years. Thank you for your life, which was full of faith in God and His Word; you are my earthly hero. You taught me that opinions mean nothing; they are just opinions. You told me to take everything to God, and that God would give me the answer through reading and studying His Word every day and developing a consistent prayer life—praying to God without ceasing.

I told you that you did not make me strong, but I recently realized that you made me spiritually tough. All the teaching, preaching, instructions, admonishments, chastisement, encouragement and so much more that you ministered penetrated my mind. God's Word is alive in my life and I am walking it out every day. I realize that you blessed me to carry the torch (mantle) like Elijah gave to Elisha. I will uphold our legacy: I will be the woman of God He made me to be. Thank you for never giving up on me, I spent more time with you than with any other person in my life. I love you dearly.

Your wife, (as you called me so affectionately, SISTER CANATLOUPE)

CONTENTS

I. Foreword

II. Acknowledgements

III. Introduction

Chapter 1. My Early Years

Chapter 2. Death of my Father

Chapter 3. Motherhood

Chapter 4. A Time of Transition

Chapter 5. Our Journey as Pastor and Wife

Chapter 6. Severe Testing and Trials

Chapter 7. My Faith Did Not Fail Me

Chapter 8. Daily Scriptures

IV. Author's Testimony

VII. Author's Biography

FOREWORD

I am truly blessed and honored to write the foreword for Dr. Jackie Kinslow's book entitled:

"I BROKE THE CURSE".

This book eloquently takes you on a journey of Dr. Kinslow's life as it relates to the challenges and trials she experienced. Her written words will bring you closer to who this dynamic woman of God is, and you will be captivated as she demonstrates in her testimony how God helped her break a multitude of curses throughout her lifetime.

Dr. Kinslow will share intimate moments of her battle with cancer. For the first time, she will put pen to paper to share the loss of her mother and sister from the same disease that plagued her life. She stands as an example who is strong in her belief in the word of God, while also depending on his powerful wonders. This woman, who broke her curse, is now a free and powerful Woman of God to bring Him glory.

I've known Dr. Kinslow for more than three decades, and when we first met, I witnessed a beloved and gracious lady who always displayed an act of kindness with a great smile. I can honestly say that I have watched her grow as she lived in pain and in hurt. Throughout these 30-plus years, she has constantly remained a kindhearted, graceful, humble, and loving lady.

Dr. Kinslow has not only been a dear friend, but she has also served as the first lady of my former Pastor, the late Eld. Arthur G. Kinslow. In 1987, I was looking for a church home and my father suggested I attend Christ Temple Apostolic Church in Pomona. I truly believe God led me, my mother and children to attend this Holy Ghost-filled church. It was there I rededicated my life back to the Lord and met this awesome sister in Christ…fondly known of as Sis. Jackie.

Over the years, no matter what she has gone through or endured, I have witnessed her commitment to the Lord. I have seen her go through many challenges and tests that would crush a nonbeliever, yet she trusted the Lord to see her through. She stands as a beacon of light for many, observing God's greatness to sustain her and to overcome the physical and mental mountains she encountered. Thank you, Jesus!

In this book, Dr. Kinslow outlines the attacks of Satan on her life. Her faith never diminished, her faith never failed her, and now she is ready to reveal to the world how she *broke the curse*. It will encourage you, bless you and bring hope to all as it was written by the love, direction, and wisdom of God.

Ephesians 3:20: Now unto him that is able to do exceeding, abundantly above all that we ask or think, according to the power that worketh in us,

DR. JACKIE KINSLOW

Pastor Jennetta Harris

J-JOY Christian Ministries, Inc.

ACKNOWLEDGMENTS

First and foremost, I am grateful to my Lord and Savior Jesus Christ, who has loved me unconditionally, even when I was unlovable. Next, I appreciate my husband, the late Suffragan Bishop Arthur Gene Kinslow, whom I had the pleasure of being married to for thirty-eight years. I cherish my one and only son, Duane Kevin Kinslow, who has always loved me and preceded me in death. I appreciate my grandchildren, Sarah (step), Tyler, Thomas and Seraiah Kinslow, who always loved me and never gave up on me. I am blessed to have my goddaughter, Nicole "Nikki" Dulaney-Millender, the daughter I always wanted, who took on the job of caring for me and handling all my affairs while I was ill. I thank God for my daughter-in-law, Tiffany Kinslow, who gave me my talented grandchildren, and I thank her for assisting me with my resume. I am thankful to God for my sister-in-love, Kathy Rolland, and my goddaughter's grandmother, Irma Dulaney, who took care of me when I was sick. I love my dear sister/friend Daisy Due of over forty years; my friend, Cindy Cotton and my close friends who keep me grounded.

I am grateful for the legacy of my grandmother, Pastor Fannie Harris, who was a pastor back in the sixties when being a woman pastor was not popular. My grandmother pastored one of the first P.A.W. churches in Zanesville, Ohio. She was a holy and consecrated Woman of God who had the gift of healing. I was told she would walk in the snow during the winter months to visit those who were sick and to pray for them and God would heal many of them. I believe I received her mantle during a church service Dr. Rachelle Benson prophesied that God had put healing in my hands and that I would help many women through their journey in life. The next Sunday when I returned to my church a visiting minister told me when I touched them, they could fill the healing in my hands, which was confirmation for the prophesy Dr. Benson gave me I am grateful to God for choosing me and using me to help many women, men and children to trust Him in every area of their lives. I thank God for my grandmother praying for my family; all my siblings are now saved, baptized in Jesus Name and filled with the Holy Ghost, my grandmother's legacy continues.

I thank God for our Church, Christ Temple Church of Pomona, Inc., and the Church Corporate Secretary Rhonda Brown who took on the laborious task of selling the church properties after the death of my husband. Thank you for working with the Secretary of the State of California and locating the non-profit organization who received the proceeds from the church property sales. Well done thou good and faithful servant.

I also thank Pastor Jenn Harris, a Holy Woman of God who prays, intercedes, and supplicates for all people. She told me on the night of my son's funeral God told her to pray for me, and she obeyed God. She knew that I lived in the city of Riverside, by one of the colleges, but she did not know which senior apartment I lived in. The Almighty God directed her, a couple of other prayer warriors, to my apartment building. They saw my husband's Mercedes in one of the parking stalls and said, "this is it." They looked at the mailboxes and found my apartment number: this was around midnight (remember Paul and Silas). They did not knock on the door; they anointed the door with blessed oil and began to cry out to God on my behalf. That was over five years ago.

The Lord brought Pastor Jenn back into my life a couple of weeks ago when I was going through many of life's challenges; she began to pray and told me exactly what I was going through. She also introduced me to a publishing company and told me she would assist me by proofreading and editing my book so that it would be in proper order for the publishing company. Let me tell you THE STEPS OF A GOOD MAN (WOMAN) ARE ORDERED BY THE LORD. (Psalms 37:23) Thank you, Pastor Jenn for your expertise.

Finally, I thank God for the mentors who graced my life, Mothers in Zion who took the time to teach and instruct me about how to become the Woman of God that I am today:

Sis. Irma Dulaney (Bishop Morris)

Sis. Daisy Due (Suffragan Bishop James)

Mother Emogene (District Elder Thomas)

Sis. Jeanette McMurray (Bishop Robert)

Mother Barbara Holman-Robinson (District Elder Robert)

Mother Geneva Smith (Bishop William)

Mother Cora Parchia (Bishop Earl)

Mother Elma Jean Bowers (Bishop Paul)

Sis. Delores Tolbert (Suffragan Bishop Grant)

Mother Esther Taylor (Bishop Charles)

Mother Janet Stewart (Bishop Carl)

Mother Magnolia Johnson (Bishop Henry)

Mother Wilma Ellis-Johnson (Bishop Henry)

Dr. Genevieve Shepherd

Dr. Norma Jackson

Dr. BJ Strother (Bishop Hershel)

Elect Lady Shirley McGriff (Bishop Donnie)

Suffragan Bishop Paulette Douglas (Bishop Robert)

Dr. Rachelle Benson (Suffragan Bishop William)

May God bless and keep all of you and may He continue to give you peace.

If the Son therefore shall make you free, ye shall be free indeed.

St. John 8:36

INTRODUCTION

This is my third book. My first book is "W.E. W.I.N.": "Women Encouraging Women In Need"; my second book is "How to Start a Church and/or Women's Ministry".

The idea for the title "I BROKE THE CURSE" came from my adopted sister-in-Christ Madeline Gulley. I was sharing how God healed me of the triple-negative breast genetic gene and that I was cancer-free. I told her that my mother and my sister died of breast cancer, and God allowed me to break the curse. She said, "That should be the title of your next book." After thinking and praying about it I decided she was right.

As I began to meditate on this title, I realized that with the help of God, I broke several curses in my life. It is my desire to share my life with you and tell you how God helped me through it all. I pray this book blesses everyone who reads it. I also pray that God will help others break the curses in their lives. God can and will deliver you, but you must allow Him to!

As I saw it, I was a statistic, and I was not supposed to succeed. The devil tried to destroy me, he tried to take my life through depression, a broken heart, illness, loneliness, desperation, and so much more. But then came Jesus, He completely changed my life. It looks something like this:

1. From my parent's divorce, to a broken home, to my father's death, to living in a children's home, to living with someone who loved me for over 38 years.

2. From being a victim of sexual abuse to becoming an overcomer and a survivor.

3. From being broken, shattered, and abandoned to being made whole, complete, single, and satisfied.

4. From becoming a ward of the court and in the foster care system to getting a good job and taking care of my son.

5. From having sex and then having a child out of wedlock to becoming celibate until marriage.

6. From not graduating from high school, to receiving a GED, Bachelor's degree, Master's degree, and Doctorate degree and becoming an ordain chaplain.

7. From multiple sexual partners to being married to one man for 38 years.

8. From my father-in-law's desire that his son not marry me and my mother-in-law thinking that that I was going to hurt her son, to becoming their best daughter-in-law, living with and caring for them until they died.

9. From having low self-esteem to realizing that I am fearfully and wonderfully made.

10. From having the spirit of fear to total faith in God.

11. From being a horrible sinner to becoming a Pastor's wife for thirty years and becoming an ordained minister of the Word of God.

12. From being a pessimist to becoming an optimist.

13. From potentially dying at the age of 49 like my father, sister, and first cousin, to celebrating my 63rd birthday.

14. From depending on others to becoming independent.

I was told that my mother was diagnosed as schizophrenic and my aunt spent time in a mental hospital; another family curse that was broken from my life. When the devil attacked my mental health, he tried his best to make me lose my mind, but God completely healed me and changed my thought process. He gave me His Spirit, which is full of power, love, and a sound mind (II Timothy 1:7).

I remember my friend Daisy telling me that I was going to beat breast cancer because my DNA was changed when I was born again. I realized that when I was baptized in Jesus's name at one of the founding churches of the P.A.W., Inc., in Columbus, Ohio, and filled with the Holy Ghost in Santa Ana California, where I attended church, I took on a new nature. I had been born again, born from above (St. John

3:3,5). The blood that Jesus shed for me on Calvary saturated my life when I believed and was baptized; I now have Jesus DNA dwelling on the inside. The sin-stained blood DNA that I received from my parents was no longer in control of my life. The blood DNA of Jesus completely and entirely washed it away. I have been crucified with Christ; nevertheless, I live by the power of the Lord Jesus Christ (Galatians 2:20). The reason why I was able to break all the curses that I was born with is Jesus Christ. He completely changed me, He adopted me into His family, I am a King's kid, I have been given all the rights and privileges of my Father, I am His child.

I have learned to trust in God with all my heart and not lean on my own understanding, but to acknowledge God in all my ways so that He can direct my path. (Proverbs 3:5-6)

God has completely transformed my life, and He has changed my mindset, teaching me how to think like He thinks. Apostle Paul said, "Let this mind be in you which was also in Christ Jesus" (Philippians 2:5). I used to think that I was so low on the totem pole, I never looked anyone in their eyes, and I was afraid to talk to anyone. I thought I was damaged goods, and I thought that I was not prideful because I did not possess anything that would make me feel proud. The Lord showed me that I had a false sense of pride, I prided myself in not having, in not being able to speak in public, in having low self-esteem. I played the victim, I had the "woe is me" syndrome, and I never learned how to forgive myself for all my sins. I tried to live a perfect life on my own. I hated myself because I kept making mistakes, I kept missing the mark.

When I sinned, I was so hard on myself, like a raped woman who feels she can wash away the effects of the rape if she takes a shower. Sin made me feel so dirty and unclean. I thought if I mentally scrubbed myself for sinning that I would not sin the next time. I thought if I punished myself for sinning that I would not do it again. I would work overtime trying to please God. The Lord told me that I was a human and humans are not perfect they make mistakes. The Lord also told me that I could not live saved on my own, but that I had to allow Him to live through me. I had to surrender my will so that His will could be done in my life, and I had to learn how to forgive myself because He forgave me when He filled me with the Holy Ghost, in August of 1976. I learned how to trust God with all my heart and lean not to my own understanding but to acknowledge Him in all my ways so that He could direct my path (Proverbs 3:5-6). I no longer feel that pressure of trying to please God by my own works, for by grace we are saved through faith, it is a gift from God.

I am a work-in-progress, and I am a witness that God can change you no matter what life brings your way. Tom Hanks as Forrest Gump said, "LIFE IS LIKE A BOX OF CHOCOLATES, YOU NEVER KNOW WHAT YOU GOING TO GET." Through Jesus Christ, we can handle any/everything that life brings our way, we can do all things through Christ which strengthens us. I thank God for always being there. He does not always deliver us from the fire of life; when He does not, He gets into the fire with us. When that test is over, we come out smelling like a rose, radiant and beautiful, and God gets all the glory out of our life.

Life is filled with all kinds of obstacles. Some we overcome, and others cause us to falter and fail. As Christians, we think God should shield us from tests and trials, but we soon realize that He does not. Salvation does not shield us from the obstacles of life, it helps us deal with life. In the end we are victorious, and we become more than conquerors through Christ who loved us and gave Himself for us.

I thank God for Reverend Milton Brunson who wrote the song "I'M FREE" The lyrics are I thank God, for I am totally free the chains have been broken, I am liberated, I am whole - mind, body, and spirit; spiritually and naturally.

I pray that this book will help all those who are going through the pressures of life, who think that their life is over, in despair, broken, shattered, diseased, lonely, abandoned, fearful, faithless, and anything else that keeps you from succeeding. God has fearfully and wonderfully made us to show the world how special we are and that He can get the glory out of our lives, no matter how humbly our lives began. There is greatness in us, all we need to do, is let God control our lives, He wants to use us and will use us as we surrender to His will. He will transform your life like He transformed mine. He changed me from a caterpillar to a butterfly and from a turkey walking around on the ground to an eagle flying high in the sky. I am soaring high above all that would distract or impede my progress.

Thank you, Sis. for allowing God to use you to give me this perfect book title: I BROKE THE CURSE. You nailed it, God bless you and thank you for being my adopted sister-in-Christ.

I will praise thee; for I am fearfully and wonderfully made; marvelous are thy works; and that my soul knoweth right well.

Psalms 139:14

Charter 1

My Early Years

God, according to His divine providence, allowed William Jackson and Martha Elisabeth Harris to give birth to their second baby girl. I was born on a hot summer day, the second of August 1958, at 7:40 pm at the Orange County General Hospital in Orange, California. According to my birth certificate, I am a Indian, part Negro mulatto. I never realized that I was an Indian. I knew that my mother's father was an Indian and her mother was white, but I never put it all together. I also heard that my father had Indian blood in his family. I was not raised by my mother, so she never told me about my heritage, and my father never mentioned it.

I often wondered why I felt like I was bougie: According to Urban Dictionary, "boujee" means, "High class, flossin', ballin'. One who possesses swag; elite and rich". But it is a stylized version of the already stylized word "bougie", which is an abbreviation of the word "bourgeois". And "bourgeois" basically means a group of people who try to adhere to a life of luxury.

I was always concerned about my appearance; I made sure that I always dressed nice; my hair had to be on point. I was never caught up with fashion, but I was very stylish. Now I realize that I have been bougie all my life.

My father, William Jackson Harris, and mother. Martha Elisabeth Harris, had six children together: Tonya, me, Jackie, Kenneth, Kim, Timothy and Russell. My sister Tonya, who was eleven months older than myself, was born breach (legs first). During delivery, her spine was broken and all the nerves in her back drew up and lodged in her spine. The doctors told my parents that she would not walk and would probably only live to be five years old. They said if she lived, she would never have children. All my parent's time was devoted to making my sister well. I was told that my father would take her from doctor to doctor lying on a pillow.

Most of my parents' time was spent caring for my ill sister; as a result I did not receive the proper love and care that I needed. When I was five years old, my father told my brother Kenneth, my sister Kim, who are twins, and me that we were going to travel to Columbus, Ohio, which was 3000 miles away to visit his mother. My father did not tell us that he and my mother were divorced and that we would not be returning to California. I didn't know this would be the last time I would see my mother for eleven years. My three other siblings remained with my mother in Santa Ana, California. Later in life when I came back to California I was reunited with Tonya, Timothy, and Russell. My sister Tonya died of breast cancer when she was 49 years old. My brother Russell was murdered in his twenties and my brother Timothy is still living in Texas.

I was also reunited with my mother when I returned to California. The relationship at first was very difficult because I blamed her for not keeping in touch with me. Over time and with the help of a good husband I forgave my mother, and we developed a sweet relationship. I had to realize my mother had her own issues to deal with and that it had to be traumatic for her to lose contact with three children she gave birth to. I learned that she did not raise my three siblings who stayed with her. They eventually ended up in foster care, so she was deprived of raising all her children. This took a toll on her and she became mentally ill, so she was not only disconnected with her children, but with most of her grandchildren as well. Later in life after we reunited, she got better, and we spent many good times together. She was diagnosed with breast cancer, after her surgery she lived approximately one year.

My father was a preaching evangelist and when we got to Ohio, he began to run revivals. He left my two siblings and I with our grandmother Fannie Harris, and we would not see him for months. One day, while we were at our grandmother's home, some of our older relatives took us upstairs into one of the bedrooms where we were introduced to sexual activities. We did not understand what they were doing but we followed their lead and it seemed like we were in that room for eternity. I found out recently when I was reunited with my siblings that this was not the first time that we had been sexually abused. We had been sexually abused before we left California, too, by one of our relatives. This activity altered our lives, robbed us of our innocence, and caused us to look at life with a distorted perception. Thank God we made it through.

My grandmother was old, and my relatives who lived with her took advantage of her, they also took advantage of us. They would partake in all kinds of devilment at my grandmother's expense. My father must have found out about it because he took us from our grandmother's house. We traveled to the countryside where he was running a revival. After his revival, he left us with an older Caucasian couple who we did not know; we stayed in their home for at least 9 months. I felt abandoned, lonely, out of place and unloved. I recently found out that the older man who we lived with molested all three of us; the sexual abuse was so traumatic for me that I didn't remember it. My brother Kenneth told me about the abuse in September of 2020.

We lived with this couple through the school the year; winter, spring, and part of the summer. They expected us to obey them without showing genuine affection or concern for us. I remember they did not have an inside toilet, only an outhouse a distance from the house, going to use the toilet was a traumatic experience coupled with a horrendous smell.

So many family and friends have taken advantage of innocent children, robbing them of their childhood' Parents need to be careful who they allow to come into their children's lives, and to keep an open communication line with their children. It would make their children's lives less complicated.

Our father finally came to pick us up, and we were happy to see him. He took us to Columbus, to live in an apartment with a lady who had two children. She was pregnant, and to our amazement, my father would sleep in this lady's room. We were confused because we already had a mother back in California.

Several months later the lady had her baby. We figured out that the baby was our father's. We began to think that our father had two wives. My father still hadn't told us that he divorced our mother—in fact, he never did tell us. And he never explained to us that he had married our stepmother and that the child she was pregnant with was his. From what I understood later, my father met my stepmother during one of his revivals. They had an affair and she got pregnant, so he married her; he was thirty-nine and she was nineteen. Our stepmother had two children, James and Louise, from a previous marriage; in the end, they had two children together, Paul and Mary.

My father was mesmerized with his beautiful young wife. We were invisible to him; he never held a conversation with us, he never interacted with us, he was present, but he was never there for us. It was like not having a father. My stepmother had no clue how to take care of seven children. I took care of my six siblings and babysat for our family and for our step-aunt's families. We were treated like second-class citizens, and the adults were treated like kings and queens; it was our job to make their lives easier. We would not be allowed to eat our meals until after the adults had eaten, and we were given a different menu than what was given to the adults. Our stepmother was our drill sergeant, and we had several regimens to complete daily before we went to school and before we went to bed.

We were in a dilemma; we lived without the love and presence of our biological mother or; the love and involvement of our father, and with an inexperienced stepmother. I later found out that our biological mother and our father did not want their children, and when they separated my father had to take three of the children and my mother kept the other three children. I was told that, while in the military, my father became unfaithful to my mother and had many sexual relationships. He was a Marine for 15 years. After retiring, he changed his life and gave his life to the Lord, repenting of his sins and receiving water baptism in Jesus Name and receiving the Holy Ghost. He gave up his extramarital affairs. Then my mother began to engage in extramarital affairs and my father would not accept this type of behavior from his wife, so he divorced her. They decided to split up the family: Tonya, the oldest who was handicapped, and the two youngest siblings, Timothy and Russell, were to stay with my mother. My father was to take me, and the twins with him. We were not told about the divorce or why we went with our father and the other siblings stayed with our mother until we were adults. This was another traumatic experience because we thought our mother didn't love us or was concerned about us.

While adjusting to our new life in Columbus, Ohio, my father, who was working at Kroger Supermarket, received a promotion and became Assistant Manager. Life began to take a positive turn. We moved from a one-bedroom apartment to a three-story duplex. Next, we moved to a two-bedroom two-story house. Then we moved to a three-bedroom upscale house in a very nice area in Columbus.

I loved to go to school, I loved learning having fun and feeling good about being in a safe environment. I was a shy young child, but education helped me to take my mind off the life I was experiencing at home. Elementary school was a breeze for me, I also enjoyed summer vacation; being able to go to the community swimming pool and all the fun times we had with our friends. I thank God for blessing me with an intelligent mind. I kept a 3.8 to 4.0 grade point average in junior high school. I remember one day during a church service, while my father was preaching he said he was proud of me for receiving good grades in school. This was the only time my father said something positive to me until the time he died. When I graduated from junior high school, I received an academic letter and was taken on the class trip to view the high school as a reward for achieving and keeping a good grade point average.

In spite of all my good grades and hard work, I had a terrible flaw. I continued to participate in sexual activity. During my early years of sexual abuse from the tender age four to seven, I experienced multiple sexual encounters, and I had multiple sexual orgasms. That sensation made me feel so good that I wanted to continue to feel that pleasure. This feeling was awakened in my life way too soon; it became my drug, and I wanted to feel that rush as often as I could. I became numb to the fact that it was sinful. Those sensations helped me to deal with my complicated life, those sensations made me feel like I was loved.

When my father and mother forsake me, then the Lord will take me up.

Psalms 27:10

Charter 2

The Death of My Father

The year I started high school was the year of many tests in my life. My father became ill, and he went to the doctor and found out he had heart problems. He had to undergo open heart bypass surgery and ended up having had a total of six bypasses. The surgery and recovery were successful. On his way home from the hospital, he wanted to drive by the church, but when he got there, he was unable to go inside as he was still weak. While at home he became lightheaded. The paramedics were called.

We were living in the projects at the time, which created its own problems: it would take the paramedics a long time to get to our house. I watched someone—I'm not quite sure who, stood my father up to put his pants on. He slumped to the floor, his eyes rolled back, and he began to swallow his tongue. Someone else grabbed a pencil and put it in his mouth. I was jumping up and down and screaming. Finally, the paramedics arrived and took my father to the hospital. I had to stay home and watch all the children. Sadly, he did not survive the night.

It was very difficult for me to accept my father's death. He had purchased a large old church, and he worked on remodeling it every day. Every Sunday after he preached, he would say "God is going to let me finish remodeling the church." When he died, I was angry and blamed God because the church was not done. At his funeral, I kept looking in the casket, expecting him to get up so he could finish it. He never got up, so I had to accept his departure from this life to transition to heaven to live with the Lord. Once I accepted it, I felt abandoned, lonely, unloved, confused, and withdrawn, and I wanted someone to love me.

I lived with my father and stepmother until my father passed in March of 1972. I was fourteen years old at the time.

After his death, my stepmother became the pastor of the church. She began to preach on Sundays, which was a surprise because we never knew that she was called to preach. One Sunday, while she was giving the Altar call, she thought that I should to come forward. Because I did not go up to the altar, she said that I was spiritually dead. This was devastating to me and for a few years I thought that I could not be saved. My stepmother allowed my brother, sister, and myself to live with her for nine months after my father's death. At the end of those months, she told us to pack all our clothes, then proceeded to take us to the municipal court. We waited outside on a bench while she went in to talk to the district attorney. I heard her tell the district attorney that she no longer wanted us. He told her that she would have to schedule an appointment for a hearing. We were not able to return home. The District Attorney handed us over to a peace officer, who took us to a detention facility to hold us because we had no home to go to. When we got to the facility, they checked us in and gave us a tour. The females stayed upstairs, and the males stayed downstairs. There was a bunk bed for each person to sleep in; about ten to a room. There were about ten showerheads in the restroom area and there were no shower curtains and no privacy. The cafeteria was downstairs, and we were scheduled to eat our first meal there at six-thirty am.

A couple of weeks later, we had a court appointment to find out where we would be placed. We became wards of the court, and the judged asked us if we knew any relatives who would be willing to take care of us. We told him we had a half-sister who lived in Zanesville, Ohio, which was about fifty-five miles from Columbus, where we currently lived. In the meantime, while we were waiting for the paperwork to go through, we stayed in the detention center and began a life without our parents. A sheriff officer drove us to our stepmother's house to get our belongings; she only allowed us to pick up our clothing, and she became the owner of the rest of our possessions. The court proceeded to get in contact with our half-sister Margaret Rush; she agreed to take care of us. A few weeks later, she came and picked us up from the detention center and we went to live with her. We remained wards of the court and stayed in the foster care system until we were 18 years of age.

A few months later, we found out that our stepmother married the funeral director who buried our father. We figured that she got rid of us because he would not take care of seven children. She kept the two children she bore with my father, but it felt like we were excess baggage that longer fit into her life.

I could still fill the pain and sting from my father's death that just happened nine months prior. This was one of the most devastating times in my life and I felt so alone and so abandoned. I also felt like no one loved me or was concerned about me and my siblings. I had so many mixed emotions and it seemed like I did not have a friend in the world.

What a life to live. As a result, I grew up thinking no one loved or was concerned about me. I have heard that we are socialized by our environment; wow that is so true. I began to develop so many phobias: fear of people and society; helplessness; flying; spiders; darkness; imperfection; failure; speaking in public, and death. I felt so lonely, and fear consumed my life.

Sex became my drug of choice because it always made me feel calm. I thought when men had sex with me that they loved me.

The steps of a good man are ordered by the Lord: and he delighteth in his way.

Psalms 37:23

Chapter 3

Motherhood

Motherhood would become a new phase of my life that no teenager can prepare themselves for. I didn't get pregnant by accident. It was an intentional decision. Looking back, I now see that loneliness will cause you to make foolish mistakes. I was still distraught about my father's passing and feeling so alone in the world that I wanted to have a child who love me unconditionally and so that I would no longer be lonely. The men in my life did not love me, they just wanted to have sex with me. I even prayed to God for a child, it was a daily prayer. I thought a child would love me and would not leave me.

One of the neighborhood young men started courting me; he tried for nine months to get me to have sex with him and I finally gave in because I saw my chance to have a baby.

A few weeks after I went to live with my half-sister, I found out that I was pregnant. This brought new problems and emotions into my life. Living with my half-sister for two months while pregnant caused my emotions to run out of control in my life. I was so depressed, so lonely, I cried all the time, and had morning sickness, I was disappointed with my life. I could not see my baby's father. I was miserable.

One day my half-sister and I had a serious argument. I decided I no longer wanted to live with her and her family. I called my caseworker and told her that I wanted to leave. I had nowhere to go, so my caseworker brought me to an unwedded mother's home. I lived there for until my son was born. This home had about twenty unwed mothers living in it. We were home schooled, we went to our scheduled doctor's appointments and we could receive outside visitors.

I felt more and more abandoned, as my boyfriend hardly ever came to see me. I remember on Mother's Day I was desperate to see him, so I checked myself out of the home and walked several miles to his house. He wasn't there and didn't come home until later that evening, so I could only spend a few hours with him. I was extremely upset with him, as I waited for him all day, but at the same time I was glad to see him.

One day I went to see my caseworker, and she told me that if I wanted to keep my son, I would need a place to stay. Being a minor, I needed an adult who was willing to allow me to live with them. I told her about my cousin, and my caseworker contacted her. God touched her heart and she agreed to let me come and live with her after the birth of the baby.

While still in the unwedded mother's home, I was all alone and had no one to sit with me through labor and delivery. I was in labor for over thirty-six hours. My boyfriend did not come to the hospital; I found out he was having sex with someone else while I was giving birth to his son.

On Saturday, September fourteenth, 1974 at ten forty-six AM, I gave birth to my BOUNCING BABY boy. The next day, my son's father Charles came to the hospital to visit us. That was one of the last times I saw him. When I was finally discharged from the hospital, I went to live with my cousin. A few months later, Charles came to see me and our son, during the visit he got angry and slapped me across my face which left his handprint on my cheek for a week. After that encounter I broke up with him and raised my son on my own. I did not give my son his father's name because I realized that I was just a sex toy to him.

My caseworker contacted a licensed babysitter, who took care of my son while I attended my eleventh year of high school. Everything seemed to be going well. However, that summer, my cousin told me that her boyfriend wanted to marry her and move to California, therefore I needed a place to live. Time for yet another move and change, so I talked to my caseworker once again and told her I had a half-sister, Sally, in Santa Ana, California she was my mother's daughter from a previous marriage, and she was 17 years older than me. God allowed my caseworker to find my half-sister and she agreed that my son and I could come live with her. The Social Service Department in Columbus, Ohio paid for my plane ticket and my son, and I traveled to Los Angeles, California. My half-sister picked us up at the airport and drove us to Santa Ana. On our way to her house, she told me she wanted me to become a model because I was so beautiful.

This was an interesting time in my life. I left the city I was born in as an innocent baby at five years old, and now I was coming back with a baby in tow. I didn't return feeling beautiful. I returned feeling like damaged goods at sixteen years old because of so many abuses in my life in such a short time.

I lived with my half-sister for a year and about three months. During that time, I was reunited with my sister and my two younger brothers, along with my three nephews and my niece.

I attended my senior year of High School in Santa Ana, California. My half-sister talked me into running for Homecoming Queen, so I ran. To my surprise, I was one of the three Princesses and served on the Homecoming Court. Before senior high school started, during the summer, my sister bleached my hair to ash blonde. Sally made my black evening gown for the Homecoming assembly and she told me to wear a white rabbit jacket. She gave me tips that would me to stand out and during the assembly; when they introduced the Homecoming candidates, I was to take the jacket off and turn around so the students could see the spaghetti straps on the back of my evening gown.

I did as she suggested, and most of the students jumped up and cheered. I was a new student and had only been there for a couple of months and they did not know who I was. They did not know me, and they could not determine what nationality I was because my hair was ash blonde, and I was light-skinned. A lot of the students voted for me because they like what I had on, I was pretty, I looked like them. I was one of three who won the nomination for Homecoming Princess.

The song leader, who was one of the three Princesses, became upset because she was not favored to win the title of Queen. She proceeded to tell her parents that I had a child out of wedlock. Her parents knew the school board members, and they threatened to take me before the school board because they felt that I should not be crowned Homecoming Queen. The school wanted to keep the peace, so they allowed the song leader to win, the Homecoming Queen title. I was so mad that I took a butter knife to the Homecoming dance, I was too scared to actually confront the winner, but I felt better with the knife in my purse. I thank God that He kept me from doing something stupid and harmful.

Later that school year, the school drama department sponsored a fashion show, and Sally once again talked me into entering the fashion show. She taught me how to model for it. I followed her instructions, and to my amazement everyone cheered and shouted when I came on stage. That was the end of my modeling experience, Sally said that I was so beautiful, and she wanted me to become a model, but that was her desire, not mine.

I finished my senior year of high school. At the end of the year I was told that I did not have enough credits to graduate, but I did get my GED a few years later.

From the time that my son was born until I left high school, I had been on welfare. Right out of high school, I got a summer youth program job. At the end of that summer, I got a new job with the Adult Work Experience Program (AWEP), where I worked for a year. After that year, the AWEP sent me to work full time as a court clerk I at a municipal court in Westminster, California. A couple of years later I became a court clerk II.

It was not easy working in Westminster. I was the only black court clerk. Every black person who worked at the Court quit because the people were so prejudiced. I was going to quit, too, but my pastor told me to stay and tough it out, so with the help of the Lord and much prayer I stayed. I won the hearts of the people, and when I quit three years later, they loved me and gave me a beautiful sendoff celebration.

Come unto me all ye that labor and are heavy laden, and I will give you rest. Take my yoke upon you and learn of me; for I am meek and lowly in heart: and ye shall find rest unto your souls. For my yoke is easy, and my burden is light.

St. Matthew 11:28-30

Chapter 4

A Time of Transition

After I finished high school and settled into my job and my new life, I began to take notice of a young man who lived across the street from my sister. We enjoyed spending time together, and soon enough we began a dating relationship. There was one problem: he wanted me to give him money. I did, thinking that he genuinely loved me. I had no clue about real love as I mentioned I thought sex was love. We were engaging in plenty of lovemaking activities, so I thought he loved me.

One day the Lord began to talk to me about salvation, I had always said that I wanted to be saved by the age of twenty-one. I was already baptized in Jesus's name, but I did not have the Holy Ghost; I was seventeen at the time. The devil told me that I still had five years to go. I began to remember those words that my stepmother told me, when she said I was spiritually dead, I am so glad I did not cling to those words real long. I began to struggle with if whether I should get saved now or wait. The Lord was encouraging me to give my life to Him and the devil was telling me to wait.

I am so glad I surrendered to the will of my Lord and Savior Jesus Christ and was filled with the Holy Ghost that summer.

While still living with my half-sister, my life drastically changed, and I told my new boyfriend, whose name was Noble, that I would no longer have sexual relations with him. He was upset and ask me to marry him. We got engaged and planned to get married, but in the meantime my cousin invited me to visit her church. I began to attend that church and became a faithful member participating in various auxiliaries. My fiancé and I began to grow apart, and I no longer wanted to marry him. He wanted me to stay with him and not to go the to the church services. I did not listen to him. I continued attending and became stronger and stronger in the faith. One day while at a missionary meeting, I asked a question regarding my engagement. One of the church mother's, told me that my fiancé was not the right person for me, as we were not on the same page, and we were unequally yoked. Thank God I listened to her and broke the engagement.

I enjoyed living for the Lord and working to support my son. My sister Tonya and I decided to get an apartment together. We filled out applications, but we were denied because we were young and unmarried, and the landlord thought we would party all the time. I discussed what I was going through with my pastor Elder Morris Dulaney, Sr. He discussed it with his wife, and they agreed to allow my son and I to move in with them. This move literally saved my life. The Pastor took me to purchase my first car, which was a 1976 white Vega with red and blue stripes. I continued to work while his wife took care of my son. While living with the Pastor and his family I was introduced to my husband, Arthur Kinslow. I was not impressed, and I quickly forgot about him.

Sometime later, while attending a youth convention, I saw Arthur sitting on the other side of the convention center and I began to feel compassionate toward him. I could not stop thinking about him and the Lord began to talk to me about him. While driving home from the convention, I told the pastor's daughter Julie, I know who I am going to marry and that it was going to be Arthur Kinslow. When we got home, she told her father, and he got in contact with Arthur. Arthur agreed to talk to me and we dated for a few months Later that year, we were engaged.

Before we got married, the Lord allowed me to find out that I had previously contracted a venereal disease. I do not know how long I had this disease, but I thank God, he allowed me to find out about it and I took medicine to clear it. I believe this disease made me sterile because my husband and I never had children together.

Arthur and I planned our wedding, and we were married a few months after our engagement on Saturday, February twenty-fifth, 1978. My son Duane was the ring bearer at our wedding. Tonya took care of Duane while Arthur and I went on our honeymoon. We traveled by car to San Francisco,

California for a week. After we returned the three of us moved into our first apartment. It was an adjustment for Duane and me as Arthur became Duane's stepfather. He was very strict, until one day Arthur's mother, Emogene, told Arthur that he was too hard on Duane, and the only thing that he would allow him to do is to go to church. Arthur listened to her, and began to include Duane by taking him on trips and allowing him to play football.

The first few years of our marriage were also challenging. Arthur was an alpha male and he wanted everything to be how he saw fit for it to be. He was the one who was in control of the family, and I had to abide by his rules. I began to loss my voice because he told me my opinions did not mean anything. I learned to be quiet because I thought that a good wife always obeys her husband. Remember, I did not grow up with good role models, so I didn't know the proper way to be a good wife. My husband told me what to do, how to do it, and when to do it. At the time I was just happy being his wife and having someone who loved me and took care of me. I was working when I met Arthur, so he allowed me to continue work, but that was not his choice for me; he didn't want me to work. My Pastor told Arthur, "If you insist that Jackie quits her job, you'll be sorry." Arthur was also a very possessive husband, and I learned how to live my life the way he wanted me to at the time. Arthur said he did not want me to become a member of his church, but that we would attend my church. He said the women at his church would eat me alive because he did not marry one of them; he was the pastor's son and a lot of the women wanted to marry him. After the wedding we remained at my church, my husband became the business manager and a deacon of the church, and I became the church secretary. The following year, the Lord called my husband into the ministry. I was not happy because I did not want to marry a minister. My father was a pastor and bishop, and I did not want that life.

Soon, I surrendered to the will of the Lord. Arthur and I enjoyed working together in the ministry, assisting whenever and wherever the need arose. We became role models for all the married couples in the church.

And he gave some, apostles; and some, prophets; and some, evangelists; and some, pastors and teachers; For the perfecting of the saints, for the work of the ministry, for the edifying of the body of Christ:

Ephesians 4:11-12

Chapter 5

Life as Pastor and Wife

Three years into our marriage, my father-in-law had a stroke that left him paralyzed on his left side. The Lord told my husband to leave our church and go back to his father's church to assist him, as he could no longer function as pastor. I was devastated, I never wanted to leave my church, but I began to pack our belongings and Duane and I traveled to Pomona to live with Arthur's parents so that he could help his mother take care of his father and become one of the assistant pastors of the church. When I asked my husband why we had to leave our church, he told me that it was well-established, and we would be of more assistance at his father's church. Again, I surrendered to the will of God. We settled into our new place of residence, and I continued working, commuting back and forth to Westminster, CA for about 5 months.

I suddenly began feeling tingling in my left arm, so I went to the doctor to find out what the problem was. He told me it was stress, and that stress was the number one cause of stroke. He asked me if there had been any recent changes in my life, so I told him that recently moved and was traveling

70 miles round trip four days a week back and forth to work. After discussing this issue with Arthur, we decided that I would quit my job. Upon my retirement I became a stay-at-home mother, assisting Duane with his homework and with anything else he needed. Duane began to meet new friends, we were happy to be together, and we enjoyed our new life.

My husband assisted his father in the ministry for almost four years, during this time we developed new relationships with the congregation. We traveled to various places as a family, and we were enjoying our lives.

One day while Duane and I were at the laundromat a thought dropped into my mind: "you are living a lie", "you never told your son that Arthur was his step-father". So, I prayed and asked God to help me tell Duane about Arthur being his stepfather, and a little about his biological father. Duane was about 10 years old at the time. He said he began to wonder because he was my ring bearer at our wedding, and he started to put two and two together.

Arthur was the only father that he knew, and he adjusted very well to the news. I previously mentioned that I prayed for a child who would love me; Duane loved me unconditionally. I thank God for my son who never stopped loving me, even though I did not know how to truly love him in the beginning. I learned how to me a good mother to Duane and a good wife to Arthur.

When my father-in-law died, my husband became the pastor of the church by the divine order of God. After my husband preached his father's Homegoing Service, the bishop got up and said that my husband would be the next pastor of the church. This was not only the bishop's desire; it was my father-in-law's desire also. He had written and signed a letter outlining his intention for his son to become the successor of the church.

Arthur, Duane and I lived with his parents from the time of his father's stroke in 1981 until his mother died in 1992. Living with my in-laws was challenging but I never complained; I was happy to go wherever my husband went because I loved him. We converted the garage into living quarters, which included two small bedrooms, a living room, a closet, and a bathroom. Our living space was quite small, but we managed, and I began to decorate.

Duane finished elementary school and junior high school, and while he was in high school, he began to play football. During this time, he developed asthma from practicing and playing on the football fields, but he wanted to play football, so he dealt with the asthma. His perseverance paid off; during a couple of the games, he was written about in the newspaper for his accomplishments.

I was so happy for Duane when he graduated high school, especially because I did not graduate, but got my G.E.D. instead.

After my father-in-law died, we continued to live with Arthur's mother for seven years. One day before my mother-in-law's death, she told my husband that she was leaving her home and all her assets to him. He told her to put her wishes in writing, then he created a living trust for her and got it notarized. After she died, we sold the house and purchased our first home in Alta Loma, CA. We lived in that home for nine years and opened it up to whoever needed a place to live, including, my brother, my niece, and two nephews for part of the time.

Two years before Arthur and I moved out of that home, Duane moved out and began his new life as an adult. During that time, he met and married his wife Tiffany, who had a daughter named Sarah from a previous relationship. Together, they had twin sons, Tyler and Thomas. I remember the first time Arthur held both of the twins. I took a picture to document this special occasion. The year after the twins were born, Tiffany and Duane had a daughter named Seraiah.

Eventually, my husband decided that he wanted to purchase me a new home. There was a new home development in Corona, CA. We put down a deposit, chose the lot that we wanted, and designed the home. We added a jacuzzi tub for the master bathroom and, a large granite island in the kitchen. We also picked out the floor tile and color of carpet. We loved our new home and lived there for ten years.

My husband became acting pastor of his father's church in July of 1985. On, October thirty-first of that same year, the district elder came to our church to meet with the board of directors about installing a permanent pastor. The Board unanimously voted for my husband, Elder Arthur Gene Kinslow. The church members were also asked to select a pastor and they unanimously voted for him.

My husband began to work on beautifying the sanctuary, and paving the parking lot. The next project was purchasing the property next door and converting it into three church offices, a fellowship room, and a kitchen, we also put a chain-link fence around the entire property. During the month of March in 1986, Bishop Robert W. McMurray, along with a host of other churches, came and installed my husband and I as pastor and wife of the church.

I told my mother-in-law I was afraid because I never wanted to be a pastor's wife, and I thought that I was not qualified. She said that I was the best candidate for the job and that God would teach me how to do it. God did that, and I became the pastor's wife that He wanted me to be.

My husband and I worked faithfully with the saints. We started a summer youth program for the children, and we fed them free lunches every day. We took the married couples on retreats, and I took the women on retreats. My husband started an Economical Development Cooperation called "For Christ's Sake," which fed, clothed, and assisted the people in the community. It had always been my desire to help women; coming from a traumatic young life, I never wanted anyone to go through what I had been through, so I started empowering women to develop new and exciting things in their lives. I inspired them to change their circumstances, to learn how valuable they were and to begin a new life with purpose and self-worth. I began to counsel women and share what I had been through, they responded, and I have been instrumental in assisting women for over 30 years. I started "W.E. W.I.N," Women Empowering Women In Need, a ministry which included helping women at the House of Ruth, a domestic violence shelter. We worked with the shelter to provide women with toiletries, bedding, toys for their children, and clothing for job interviews. We also provided makeovers.

Approximately five years after becoming pastor, my husband was elevated to District Elder of District # 12 in Southern California under the leadership of Bishop Robert W. McMurray, and thirteen churches were placed under our jurisdiction. A few years later the California-Nevada-Hawaii Council, which we belonged to, divided and we became members of the newly formed Southern California Area # 1 Council. My husband was appointed Council Treasurer and I was appointed Ministers and Deacons Wives Vice President under the leadership of Bishop Charles and Lady Esther Taylor.

My husband and I were also active members of our parent organization, the Pentecostal Assemblies of the

World, Inc., holding various positions and traveling throughout the country. We served under the leadership of Bishop Robert W. and Lady Jeanette McMurray, Bishop Charles L. and Lady Esther Taylor, Bishop Henry and Lady Magnolia Johnson and Bishop Robert and Lady Paulette Douglas in the state of California.

I was called and anointed by God to declare His Word. When God called me, He kept coming to me saying "I HAVE ANOINTED YOU TO PREACH THE GOSPEL…" (Luke 4:18) I did not want to hear the Lord, so I ran from the call. God would not leave me alone; He did not accept the excuses I gave Him. Months later I surrendered to the call of God. You will not be happy until you surrender your will to God's will. Just like Jesus said in the Garden of Gethsemane: "NEVERTHELESS NOT MY WILL BUT THY WILL BE DONE" (Luke 22:42). When God has a call on your life, you are going to fulfil that call, if you do not you will live a life of total confusion and you will go through unnecessary trials. Once you surrender, God's peace will cover you and you will become who God wants you to be. We must remember that God places us in the body as it pleases Him. He is the one who is in complete control.

I told Arthur about the call that God placed on my life, and he told me that there was only going be one minister in our family. Therefore, I told him that God called me to develop a ministry that taught/instructed the Word of God. After much praying, God changed his heart. My husband accepted that God called me to preach and I began to preach/teach and assist him in the ministry at our local church. A few years later he asked me if I wanted to take over the church, I told him God did not call me to pastor. Even so, my husband taught me how to successfully operate just about every position in the church.

Despite all the challenges, tests, trials, and disappointments, that came with our work, we enjoyed working together, and we realized that God brought us to the kingdom for such a time a this.

But the God of all grace, who hath called us unto his eternal glory by Christ Jesus, after that ye have suffered a while, make you perfect, stablish, strengthen, settle you.

I Peter 5:10

Chapter 6

Severe Testing and Trials

The next several years would prove to be full of severe testing and trials. No one could make these things up, and as I wrote this chapter, I continued to reflect on the grace of God.

One Sunday after church I drove my grandchildren to their home and Duane came out to talk to me. I noticed that he looked very tired. He drove a gravel truck and I thought he was just tired from working so hard. But he did not look well to me, so I prayed for him. The next day I was talking to a friend and a call beeped on my phone, immediately my motherly instincts kicked in and I thought, this is my son and he is sick. I answered the call and was told to stop everything and get to Kaiser; something was wrong with Duane's kidneys. Arthur and I traveled to Kaiser and went to the emergency room where Duane was being examined. We were with him when the doctor told Duane that we had to go on dialysis because his kidneys were only working at 2 percent, meaning they were completely shut down. Because he was a truck driver, he had to get regular checkups. For a few years they mistook his high blood pressure for the source of what was wrong with him. But his kidneys were the reason why he was having high blood pressure. Duane remained in the hospital until all the toxins were cleaned out of his body.

After Duane was released from the hospital, he began dialysis treatments three times a week, which was not enough, as his kidneys were not functioning at all. Tiffany questioned why Duane only received three days of treatments per week. The doctors told her the insurance companies only allow dialysis patients to receive three treatments per week because of the cost. Tiffany researched and found a new company in Texas that made portable dialysis machines for the home. Duane and Tiffany had to attend a six-week training session to learn how to operate the machine. Once they started using the new machine Duane's health began to improved. The company was so impressed that they hired Duane to sell their products, he was very successful.

Duane was a people person. Everybody liked him. His doctor liked him so much that she was instrumental in getting Duane a new kidney within a short time. Duane received his new kidney from San Diego Medical Center. He recovered and continued to be successful.

A few years later, the year 2012 started off very well. My husband and I were enjoying life, my son was successful in his career, and my grandchildren were growing up fast. Life was peaceful, and we were finally able to enjoy our dream home.

In January, we were planning out our year and our finances, and it was at this junction that we decided to refinance our home. After completing the paperwork, we emailed the documents right away to the refinance company. A few weeks went by, and my husband called the loan company only to hear them say they did not receive the documents. We emailed the documents again a second time, and the same thing happened again. We continued to go through this process over the next several months. This was during a time when the country was having problems with loan companies and people were losing their homes in droves. One day the loan company called to advise my husband they were working on the refinancing of our home, so we began to feel at ease that things were moving along. We left the house later that day to only return home to find a letter on our front door. It was a notice advising us that we had two weeks to vacate the property because our home was in foreclosure. We had to pack everything and leave our dream home. We were devastated.

Once we left our dream house, we were homeless, and we had to rent a moving van to put our furniture in and then make reservations to stay in a hotel. It was hard trying to find somewhere to live because we had a foreclosure on our credit report. We finally found a house to rent in Adelanto, California which was an hour away from our church. The rental agency rejected our offer, and we went back to our hotel room still in need of a permanent place to live. I turned on the TV and listened to The Word Network. The pastor was preaching, saying, "go back and ask them again." I shared this message with my husband, and we drove back to Adelanto and spoke again to the real estate agent about the rental property. The Lord moved upon his heart and the gentleman changed his mind and decided to allow us to lease the house.

This house was about half the size of our dream home, but we were glad to have a place that we could call home. I began to decorate our new place to make it beautiful and comfortable as we adjusted to our new environment.

It took us an hour to drive to church with the amount of traffic commuting up and down the Cajun Pass, but God kept us covered with His blood and we never had an accident. To God be the glory. After living in Adelanto for a year and traveling through the Cajun Pass on a consistent basis I became physically and mentally drained, so we decided to move.

While we were having a moving sale the summer of 2013, our daughter-in-law let us know that Duane was in the hospital in Las Vegas. His kidneys had failed again. We packed up and drove to Las Vegas. When we got to our son's room he could not speak; he had suffered a stroke. The doctor said that part of his brain function was destroyed and that he had to learn how to walk and talk again. We began to pray. My husband stood beside by Duane's bed and began talking to him. When he told him "I love you," my son bellowed out a horrible cry because he could not talk.

Later that day Tiffany and I went to go get something to eat, and while we were at the restaurant, we received a call from my husband. He said that Duane was talking; God had performed a miracle. When we returned to the hospital, my son wanted to walk around: another miracle. He walked around the entire hospital floor. Everybody was rejoicing. People all over the country prayed for our son and God answered their prayers; what a mighty God we serve. Duane was a backslider, and while he was in the hospital he repented and got his life straight.

Unfortunately, he had to go back on dialysis. Shortly after, he was released from the hospital, his home life became unbearable, and he had relapse and started living a life that was contrary to the Word of God. Duane and his wife's martial problems escalated and to keep the peace he decided to leave, so he departed from his marriage. Duane moved out, and relocated to Stockton, CA, the beginning 2014. One of the reasons why he moved so far was because he found out that he had cancer and he did not want me and his children to know that his health was deteriorating. Several months after he moved, he called me, during our conversation he began to apologize for everything he had done wrong throughout his life. I forgave him and God also forgave him. I believe he realized that he only had a short time to live, the kidney disease and cancer had taken its toll on his life, and he wanted to make sure everything was in order.

The fall of 2013, while preparing to move, I began to feel nervous, I prayed and fasted, but this feeling would not go away. I continued to teach and preach and to perform all my duties at home and at church. We started looking for a place to live, we found a senior apartment complex in Riverside. We filled out the application and gave it to the property management worker. She reviewed the application and advised us that it was rejected. After a few days, my husband went back and talked with the property management worker, and they came up with an agreement to allow us to move in. We moved into our apartment November 2013, right before Thanksgiving. We so happy and I decorated the apartment, as this was one of my many pleasures.

Even after moving in and decorating, I continued to be stressed and nervous; I lost my appetite, and I could not sleep. I began to feel anxious, and it turned into anxiety. Fear began to set in, and I was afraid of leaving the house. I was still praying, reading the Word of God, studying but nothing stopped this downward spiral. I became weak and the devil began to talk to me, telling me that I did not have faith. That made me become severely depressed and I lost hope. My mind became confused, constantly running, never stopping. It became hard to get out of the bed. I was eating only one meal a day. I was afraid to eat, thinking I would throw up everything that I ate. I stopped going to church and I was in torment every day, a year had passed, it was now the end of the summer in 2014. The devil constantly told me to take my life. He would tell me to walk away, leave the house, run away and I run away several times, but each time I ran away the Lord would allow me to find my way back home.

I became so depressed that Arthur thought I was going to die, so he called Duane and told him to come and visit me right away. Duane came to see about me and asked me what was going on. I told him my mind was not functioning properly. When he left that day, he told Nikki, my Goddaughter, that he recognized that something was wrong because I was folding the towels in a different way. He came back the next day, but I was so tired and confused that I did not get out of the bed. He came into my room right before he left to tell me goodbye. That was the last time I saw him. Three months later, in September of 2014, Duane died.

By that time my mind was very confused, and I could not feel any emotions. I could not cry; my tears ducts dried up. I did not have any kind of fear. I was told that Duane had died, but I could not feel anything. The day of his funeral, my stomach was hurting so bad that I could not get out of the bed. As I look back on that day, I am mortified that I did not attend his funeral. I did not mourn his death until I was healed of the mental illness.

Mental illness robs you of everything that is important to you. I am so glad that I got help; I went to receive counseling from a psychiatrist, and she helped me to begin my healing process. I thank God for allowing me to have my son. He lived for 39 years, God answered my prayer and gave me someone who loved me unconditionally. I will always cherish his memory. After the death of Duane, I became clinically depressed and it was hard for my husband to accept my mental illness He cried, which was something that he did not do. He would beg me to get up, he said that he wished that he had handled things differently when it came to how he had treated me throughout the early stages of our marriage. Yet by now the damage was already done. Back then, my husband was an alpha male and he had to be in complete control. I gave up my life and surrendered to his will doing almost everything he told me to do. Whenever we had a disagreement, I would be the one who would bring harmony back into our marriage. I would always be the one who said I am sorry, even if he was the cause of the disagreement. He told me that he hated to say he was sorry while growing up. He told me that I taught him how to say, "I am sorry."

Arthur learned how to love me unconditionally after he became pastor back in 1985. He began to study the Bible differently and learned his role as to how a husband was to take care of his wife. The Bible says in chapter five of the book of Ephesians "Husbands, love your wives, even as Christ also loved the church, and gave himself for it." Arthur taught a Bible series on the family, and after teaching that series he began to respect me and love me in a different way. He began to nurture and cherish me and respect my opinions. From that time our marriage began to blossom, and everyone began to tell us that we were the perfect couple.

Arthur had always been a fixer, he tried to fix me, he wanted me to get better; when this did not happen and he could not fix me, he began to think that he was a failure. He told me, "if I cannot help you, I cannot help anybody." I tried to get better but I could not; I was so damaged mentally that everything I tried to do to get better did not help me; I only grew worse. This broke Arthur's heart, because I stayed in the bed most of the day and only ate one meal. I lost almost one hundred pounds in a very short time.

While I was in the bed nursing my mental illness, the California District Council, which we were members of, was divided into three new Councils and received three new bishops. We were placed in the Central California District Council under the leadership of Bishop Robert and Lady Paulette Douglas, and Arthur was elevated to Suffragan Bishop. I was sick and was unable to attend the celebration. Arthur honored and served Bishop Douglas faithfully and he was also an example to all the church leaders. I was also unable to attend Arthur's Installation Service. By this time, he was dealing with his own illness.

My husband had high blood pressure for most of our marriage; it was over 200 every day, and that took its toll on his life. He became ill; his legs began to swell, they cracked, and fluid began to flow out. Then his skin started to come off. His legs wept fluid for months and all the flesh came off both of his legs, He would wrap them up with sterile gauzes when he left the house. He could not sleep; the fluid was filling up in his body. He lost, his appetite and lost a lot of weight.

He did not want to go to the doctor; he told me this throughout our marriage. He made me promise that I would never take him to the doctor, saying "if God does not fix it, it doesn't need to be fixed." He remained faithful to his testimony; he trusted in God until the end and took his final breath on Thursday morning before dawn on June 25, 2015.

I had gotten little sleep when I woke up and came into the living room to check on him. Deacon Eugene had been helping me take care of him for almost two weeks, and he was with my husband. Arthur's breathing was labored, and as we were watching him, he took what we both knew was his last breath. The Deacon called the paramedics. They came and worked on him for about twenty minutes before pronouncing him deceased. Then the coroner came and took his body.

Arthur did not want a funeral; he told our goddaughter Nikki that he did not want anything and that if she had something for him, he would come back and haunt her. So, there was no service for Arthur. He had also decided that upon his demise that the church where he pastored would be dissolved. The Board of Directors meeting a few years before his death, in which the Board unanimously voted that on the demise of the pastor the church would be dissolved because there was no one in the congregation to fill the pastoral position. My husband did not want someone else to come in and change the standards that his father established as the founder of the church. The church was dissolved in accordance with the Secretary of the State of California. All the proceeds were given to a 501© 3 organization. When the church property was sold, I did not receive any of those proceeds; my husband took care of business and took care of me through his life insurance. I thank God that my husband prioritized the life insurance no matter what happened in our lives; even when we did not have money to pay our mortgage, my husband would pay his life insurance bill.

After the death of my husband, I did not grieve right away, I was mentally distressed and confused. My emotions were completely shut down, I could not cry, my tears were dried up and I was numb. My mind was so confused that nothing bothered me; I did not have any feelings. My new pastor, Morris Dulaney, Jr., said that I was a walking zombie. I was so weak spiritually, mentally, and physically. The Devil was constantly talking to me, telling me that I did not have faith; I began to believe him. When a person does not have faith, they lose hope, and when you lose hope, you lose your desire to live so my desire was to die. The Devil kept telling me that everyone would be better off if I died. I tried to take my own life, but the Lord would not allow me to be successful. The Lord kept telling me "You shall live and not die and declare the works of the Lord". (Psalms 118:17)

My sister-in-love came to stay with me after my husband died; this gave my goddaughter a break, and she was able to go back to work; she would visit me after she got off work every day. My sister-in-love took care of me, and I will always be grateful for her love and concern about me. One day the Devil told me to run away, so I left and hid myself at this pond area not far from the house. I was there all day. The Lord spoke to me and told me to go back home, so I did. When I got home, my sister-in-love called my goddaughter, and she came and told me that we were going to the hospital. We traveled to the hospital, where they gave me a complete physical and, a prescription to calm down my nerves. My goddaughter told me that she was going to check me into a mental facility; we checked in and had to wait for them to admit me. There were so many mentally ill people waiting to be admitted, and I was so afraid. My goddaughter looked at me and said, "do you want to stay here?" I replied, *"NO."* We left, stopped by Jack-in-the-Box to get something to eat, and drove back home.

After this traumatic experience and the possibility of staying at a mental facility, the next day my goddaughter scheduled to take me to a psychiatrist. I went to see the psychiatrist every two weeks and she helped to start me on my road to recovery. At the time I did not have medical insurance, so I had to pay the doctor $200.00 per visit. My goddaughter was able to secure medical insurance for me, therefore I changed doctors and was assigned a new psychiatrist and, a psychologist. I had appointments with these two doctors every two weeks, and they took me step-by-step through the process of dealing with my past. My doctor told me that I had been in survival mode since I was five years old and that my past was so traumatic that my mind completely shut down because the pressure was so great. All three of my doctors were Christians and, they helped me tremendously. I remained in my severely depressed state for four years losing about one hundred pounds because it was hard for me to eat. I was afraid to eat, the depression made it hard to swallow and I would almost vomit the food I ate every time I would eat. My mind never rested, it was hard to sleep, I would doze off and wake back up shortly after I went to sleep. I was in a miserable state of mind. My doctors tremendously helped me with my mental health issues, assisting me each session to get better. My psychiatrist mentioned she was going to wean me off the medication. I was told once you start taking those medications you will never get off them but by the grace of God, the doctor did something that she never does; she weaned me off the meds, HALLELUJAH. I was only on them for three years. Both of my doctors released me from my sessions because they saw what God had done for me. I am free, thank God I am free.

After Arthur died, my god-daughter Nikki, asked me if I was willing to move in with her grandparents, I agreed. She said that my husband told her that if anything happened to him that he did not want me to live alone. Two months after I moved in, my stomach began to bother me and the pain was so severe, I asked the bishop to pray for me. He did, but the pain would not go away. I was asked if I was willing to go to the doctor, and I agreed. We went to urgent care, where the doctor told me I had a bladder infection and, ran some other tests. Before we arrived home, the doctor called and left a message saying that I needed to go to the hospital. We went the next morning, and the attending doctor told me that he was going to admit me to the hospital. I had jaundice; my gall bladder was infected. If had waited one more day I would have died.

I was admitted and scheduled for gall bladder surgery. While I was in surgery, they discovered that my bile ducts were inflamed; they could not understand why the poison did not get into my blood stream. The doctor said that my gall bladder had been infected for years. He also said that he had been a doctor for twenty-five years and that he had never seen a gall bladder so infected. God kept His arms of protection around me, Glory to God. What a miracle. They also said that I did not have any medical insurance even though, we had applied for it, but the next day they said that I was approved, so I was covered. God continued to do great things for me. After they repaired my bile ducts, they removed my gall bladder.

I thank God for Nikki and her grandmother Irma for taking care of me while I was sick. They made sure that I ate three meals a day, they made me walk, and they sometimes got me out of the bed to sit in the family room. The road to recovery was long and hard, yet I know My God is an Awesome God and He took me through the healing process each step of the way. I realized that the Devil was lying to me, I did have faith, I never blamed God, I never cursed God, I never said why me, I blamed myself. God never left me nor forsook me, He continued to work things out for me. I was told that I read the Word of God every day, I am sure that it helped me through the process.

And the Lord said, Simon, Simon, behold, Satan hath desired to have you, that he may sift you as wheat: but I have prayed for thee, that thy faith fail not: and when thou art converted, strengthen thy brethren.

Luke 22:31-32

Chapter 7

My Faith Did Not Fail Me

The beginning of 2018, I began to watch Word of Faith's livestream. The more I tuned in to their online services, the more the Lord began to strengthen me, and my faith in God revived. One Sunday, the pastor told the saints to go on a fast for three days: Wednesday through Friday. On that Friday, which was Good Friday, we would take communion during the service. I decided to participate in the fasting, then I decided to attend the service. The service was just what I needed, so I decided to go to Resurrection Sunday Service. On that day I repented, and have remained faithful to God, growing in His Grace and knowledge.

The Lord restored my joy, peace, happiness, prayer life, studying and praying. I began to preach and, teach again and my faith exploded. God let me know that I never lost my faith. It never failed me, even though I had gone through a time of testing and trials. He reassured me that He never left me nor forsook me; He was there all the time. My mustard-seed faith sustained me throughout all the hurt, pain and trials.

I am so grateful, thankful, and appreciative to God for saving me, changing me, regulating my mind, taking out my stony heart and giving me a heart of flesh. I completely trust in God. I have totally surrendered to the will of God, I am free and no longer bound, I have no more chains holding me, I am fearfully and wonderfully made by God. He is my God, Father, husband, friend, King, Lord, Redeemer, Reconciler, Shepherd, Savior, Healer, way-maker, provider, everything that I need Him to be and so much more.

After my sixty-first birthday on, August second, 2019, the devil went to God and said that he wanted to test my faith again, and God allowed him to test me spiritually, naturally, socially, and financially. I successfully passed every test, so the devil asked God if he could attack my life and he did.

The next month, September, I went to the doctor because I had severe back pain. The doctor gave me a muscle relaxer and told me to come back the following week. When I returned, the doctor told me to go get a mammogram while was there. The results determined that I had a mass in my left breast. After this, I had to get a sonogram, an ultrasound, and another mammogram. A week later I was told that I had breast cancer. I was not afraid, for God revealed to me that the cancer was not unto death.

I informed my church family, and the pastor told the ministers to pray for me. One of the ministers laid her hands on the area where the cancer was. The next day I went to see the surgeon. He told me that the cancer and was aggressive kind It had been in my body for five to six years, but they caught it during its earliest stage. It was a miracle, for it had not grown in those five to six years.

I asked the doctor if he could test me as I believed that God had already healed me. The doctor told me the only way I would find out was when he operated on me, and he continued to say, "I love the Lord too." When I asked him why he said this, he replied, when people tell me that they go to church, they think that God is going to heal them, and they do not want to have the surgery they need." Arthur always told me, "if you go the doctor, do what the doctor says" so I planned to obey the doctor I told him I would have the surgery, and he calmed down and explained that most people never come back when he told them they have cancer. He thought I was not going to listen to him or take his advice. When he realized that I was going to go through with the surgery he changed his tone and he was very nice to me.

He told me that I needed to be tested to see if I have a genetic predisposition for cancer since my mother and sister died of breast cancer. The doctor also advised me that if I did have the cancer gene, it would be necessary for him to remove both of my breasts. I had the genetic test the same day, and the specialist told me it would take four weeks to get the results. To my surprise, the Lord allowed them to return the test results in one week. I received a call and was told that the results were negative. God healed me of the breast cancer gene.

The surgery was scheduled immediately, and as I began to mentally prepare for this procedure, my faith rose even more. I asked the Lord to prove to the doctor that God was in control, and by all accounts, the Lord manifested Himself, in that the surgery only required a removal of lymph nodes and cancerous tissue… and my breast remained intact. From the onset, the doctor thought he may have to remove both breasts, but by God's Amazing Grace… it was not so. I went to my follow-up appointment and the doctor was so excited to see me that he came into the examining room right away. He told me he removed the cancerous tissue, some lymph nodes, and some extra tissue. He said the cancer did not spread, and in his words, "we got all the cancer."

As I began my chemotherapy, I asked the Lord to allow me to keep my appetite, enhance my taste buds, to continue to walk, to keep me well, and not become tired. The Lord answered my prayer and did just that. I had eight chemo treatments over a period of five months; one of the side effects for the type of chemo I received was hair loss. It was on a Sunday evening after the second treatment that I started combing my hair and noticed that a lot of hair was in the comb. I took the hair out of the comb and continued to comb my hair and more and more hair came out. I took my hands through my hair and more hair continually came out. I was devastated, and I began to cry as I felt like my womanhood was leaving me. I had breast cancer, and my hair, which at the time was all the way down my back, was my pride and joy, and I did not want to be bald. I had to regroup, calm down, trust the process, and most importantly trust that God knew what He was doing. I decided to have my hairdresser shave off the rest my hair and when I looked in the mirror it did not look as bad as I thought. I accepted my fate and became brave enough to show my bald head. Some of my friends told me that I still looked pretty, and I praise God every day for hair restoration.

The type of breast cancer that I had was triple negative breast cancer and not the normal type of breast cancer. I had three different chemo cocktails; one was so toxic that they manually administered the treatment to prevent any flow outside of my bloodstream. After receiving my chemo treatments, which lasted over the period of six months, I had a post-treatment telephone call with her my oncologist she asked me, why "I had been so quiet." I asked her what she meant, and she said, "You have not called or asked questions about problems or symptoms." I told her because did not have any questions or concerns.

She explained that most people who receive chemo treatments become nauseated, very tired, have problems with eating and keeping their food in their stomach, and are not able to functions like they desire to, and they have a lot of questions and are constantly calling their oncologist for assistance. I explained to her: I prayed and asked God to keep me well through the chemo treatments; to let me be able to continue to walk five days a week; to be able to keep my appetite not get nauseated, and He honored my request. He also added something that I did not ask, my tasted buds were enhanced, and I could taste most of the spices in every dish of food I ate. This is not a normal thing for cancer patients.

The doctor replied, "That's God, because you had triple negative breast cancer. It has the worst prognosis, it's the hardest cancer, and the treatment is more powerful and harder on patients." She "also told me she was surprised that I was already receiving radiation treatments, because she felt the doctor didn't give me time to rest." I let her know that he gave me a month to rest before treatments.

As we continued with my checkup call, the doctor turned the conversation toward me. She started testifying to me about me. She said, "That is because the radiologist knows that you are strong". She said, "when you are diagnosed with cancer, you do not get strong during the cancer, you would have to be strong before you were diagnosed". My oncologist recognized that God helped me to make it through a very trying time without their assistance. That was the only way I could have made it through. Many people die when they have cancer, but God allowed me to make it through, and the doctors knew that God assisted me. Thank you Jesus, she was right, and I completely trusted in God through it all.

The doctors never told me the type of breast cancer I had until after I was almost finished with my procedures. When I got home, I looked up "triple negative breast cancer," and read that this type of cancer is not hormonal, and it comes from your mother or your father. Earlier in this chapter I said that after the ministers prayed for me and God healed me. The test proved to me and to the doctors that I had been healed. My oncologist was so amazed that she said, "we need to do a case study on you."

I thank God for choosing me to go through this type of cancer to show the world that He is still in control. It is documented and recorded for all the world to see that my God is Phenomenal, Awesome, Amazing, Incredible and that He is the True and Living God who can heal everything in our lives.

When I had my three-month follow-up checkup with my surgeon, everything looked good. I asked him, what the difference was between being cancer-free, and cancer in remission. I learned from him that when cancer in remission, you still have the cancer, and it has metastasized, but it goes to sleep and stops spreading. He also explained that", cancer-free," means that the surgeon removed all the cancer during the surgery, and the cancer did not spread. He said, "I got all the cancer out of your body, and you are cancer-free."

HALLELUJAH, GOD SHOWED THE DOCTOR THAT HE WAS IN CONTROL. The doctor was amazed, and I was excited that God performed a miracle in my life.

2020, has been an eventful year so far, and God gave me a word of knowledge at the last service of the year 2019. I was testifying to God's glory, and I began to utter words as to how 2020 will not be what everyone is proclaiming that it to be. God gave me a word and I shared with the congregation that 2020 would be different. My prediction was not received in the spirit which it was given but God knows the ending from the beginning, and He knew the year 2020 was going to change our lives.

When the world found out that there was a pandemic (Corona virus 2019, known as Covid-19), I was not surprised at all, as God is in complete control, and He knew this pandemic was going to happen before the foundation of the world. God is coming back soon, and He is using this pandemic to help the church to prepare themselves for the Rapture. He is coming back soon, only those who are ready will make it in the great catching away.

The Bible tells us to "Occupy 'til He comes" (Luke 19:13) so I decided to take an online class to receive my Chaplain Certificate and badge. The class was inspiring, uplifting, eye-opening, encouraging and on-point. In the second week of July, 2020, I received my graduation certificate, ordination ceremony, and official badge for chaplaincy. To God be the Glory for the things that He has done. I plan to get a job as a chaplain, assisting people who are in need. I WILL LIVE AND NOT DIE AND DECLARE THE WORKS OF GOD. (Psalms 118:17) I also plan to get my own place of residence, and I cannot wait to decorate it. I am so excited about the next chapter in my life and about everything that God is going to do for me. I have sown good seeds and my harvest is on the way. By the way, I did move from Corona to San Diego. This is the first time that I have ever lived by myself, and I love it.

I encourage everyone who reads my story to put your complete trust in God. He knows our end from our beginning, and He loves us unconditionally. He knows the way we take, and when He has tried us, we shall come forth as gold. One of my favorite scriptures states "Favor is deceitful and beauty is vain: but a woman that fears the Lord, she shall be praised. Give her the fruit of her of her hands; and let her own works praise her in the gates." (Proverbs 31:30-31)

My God who I serve has completely changed everything in my life: **Spiritually,** he helped me to realize that I needed to be saved from a life of sin; I was shaped in iniquity, and in sin did my mother conceive me (Psalms 51:5). I was baptized in Jesus name for the remission (completely washing away) of my sins (Acts 2:28), and I was filled with the Holy Ghost (Acts 2:4). **Naturally** he taught me that I am fearfully and wonderfully made; I am more than a conqueror and that I am blessed and highly favored. **Mentally** He let me know if I keep my mind stayed on Him He will keep me in perfect peace; He told me to think on things that are true, honest, just, pure, lovely and that I can do all things through Christ who strengthens me (Philippians 4:8,9,13) and **Financially** He told me if I paid tithes and offerings He will always take care of me (Malachi 3:10-12). God assisted me in breaking every curse in my life. He gave me a new outlook on life, He changed my direction, He gave me hope and increased my faith. I love Him with all my heart, soul, mind, and strength.

What He did for me, He is ready and willing to do it for you and will do it, all you have to do is to have faith and obedience, you can cast (throw) all your cares (weaknesses, infirmities) upon Him, for He cares (continues to care) for you (I Peter 5:7). I love, pray, and wish above all things that you prosper and be in health, even as your soul prospers (III John 2).

As I look back from the time I was four years old, and the pain that began at such young age, to having a child at 16, to the many places I resided, to the pain and grit of losing my only baby boy, Duane, to losing my husband of 38 years, to the illness, that found their way in my body, to my being stricken with four years of depression and to my test with cancer… with God's help… I Broke the Curse of it all. No longer will any of these things haunt me, because the Lord has kept me and covered me through it all. For that, I say, Thank You Jesus for keeping me every step of the way. MY FAITH DID NOT FAIL ME.

All scripture is given by inspiration of God, and is profitable for doctrine, for reproof, for instruction in righteousness: That the man of God may be perfect, thoroughly furnished unto all good works.

II Timothy 3:16-17

Chapter 8

Daily Scriptures

In this chapter I will share with you some of the scriptures that I quote every day. These scriptures have made me spiritually wealthy, and I call them my golden nuggets. I quote them, believe in them, and live them. They have given me abundant, eternal, and everlasting life; they keep me energized. The Word of God contains God's mind, will and volition. God does not speak outside of His Word. His Word is our road map to heaven. The bible says, "Beloved, believe not every spirit, but try the spirits whether they are of God: because many false prophets are gone out into the world (I John 4:1)." Every spirit that comes to your mind or that you hear is not always God. You must try the spirits by the Word of God. If you do not know how to search the Word of God pray and ask Him to help you. He said, "If any man lack wisdom, let him ask God that giveth to all men liberally and upbraids not." (James 1:5). God will lead and guide you to all truth, for He is good like that. The following scriptures are proof that God will help you, I have committed these scriptures to memory, and I quote them every day. I pray they bless you as they have me.

Faith cometh by hearing and hearing by the Word of God. (Romans 10:17)

Now faith is the substance for things hoped for, the evidence of things not seen. (Hebrews 11:1)

But without faith it is impossible to please him, for he that cometh to God must believe that he is and that he is a rewarder of them that diligently seek him. (Hebrews 11:6)

Forever O Lord thy Word is settled in heaven. (Psalms 119:89)

Thy Word is a lamp unto my feet and a light unto my path. (Psalms 119:105)

Man does not live by word alone, but by every word that proceeds out of the mouth of God. (Deuteronomy 8:3)

All scripture is given by inspiration of God and is profitable for doctrine, for reproof, for correction, for instruction in righteousness. That the man of God may be perfect, thoroughly furnished unto all good works (II Timothy 3:16-17)

No prophecy of the scripture is of any private interpretation. (II Peter 2:21)

Sanctify them through thy truth, thy Word is truth. (St. John 17:17)

Study to show thyself approved unto God a workman that needs not to be ashamed, rightly dividing the Word of truth. (II Timothy 3:16)

Trust in the Lord with all thine heart and lean not to thy own understanding. In all thy way acknowledge the Lord and he shall direct thy path. (Proverbs 3:5-6)

For God so loved the world that he gave his only begotten Son, that whosoever believeth in him should not perish, but have everlasting life. (St. John 3:16)

And we know that all things work together for good to them that love God, to them who are the called according to his purpose. (Romans 8:28)

For I know the thoughts that I think towards you... thoughts of peace and not of evil to bring you to an expected end. (Jeremiah 29:11)

But the God of all Grace, who hath called you unto his eternal glory by Christ Jesus, after you have suffered a while shall make you perfect establish, strengthen, and settle you. (I Peter 5:10)

Looking unto Jesus the Author and Finisher of our faith, who for the joy that was set before him endured the cross despising the shame and is set down on the right hand of God. (Hebrews 12:2)

For we have not a High Priest which cannot be touched with the feeling of our infirmities but was tempted in all points like as we are, yet without sin. (Hebrews 4:15)

Whatsoever things are true, whatsoever things are honest, whatsoever things are just, whatsoever things pure, whatsoever things are lovely, whatsoever things are of good report; if there be any virtue and if there be any praise, think on these things. Those things, which ye have both learned and received and heard and seen in me, do and the God of peace shall be with you. (Philippians 4:8)

I can do all things through Christ which strengthens me. (Philippians 4:13)

Beloved now are we the sons of God and it does not appear what we shall be, but we know that when he shall appear, we shall be like him for we shall see him as he is. And every man that hath this hope in him purifies himself even as he is pure. (I John 3:2-3)

And this is the confidence that we have in him, that if we ask anything in his will, he heareth us. And if we know that he hears us we know that we have the petition that we desired of him. (I John 5:14-15)

He that dwelleth in the secret place of the Most High, shall abide under the shadow of the Almighty. I will say of the Lord he is my refuge and fortress, my God in him will I trust. Surely, he will deliver thee out of the snare of the devil, he shall cover thee with his feathers and under his wings shalt thou trust. His truth shall be thy shield and buckler. Thou shalt not be afraid of the terror my night, nor for the arrow that fly by day, nor for the pestilence that walketh in darkness, nor for the destruction that wastes at noonday. A thousand shall fall at thy side and ten thousand at thy right hand but it shall not come nigh thee. Only with thy hands shalt thou see the reward of the wicked. (Psalms 91:1-8)

The Lord is my Shepherd, I shall not want, he makes me to lie down in green pastures, he leadeth me beside the still waters, he restoreth my soul. He leadeth me in the path of righteousness for his namesake. Yea, though I walk through the valley of the shadow of death I will fear no evil. Thou anoint my head with oil my cup runs over. Surely, goodness and mercy shall follow me all the days of my life and I will dwell in the house of the Lord forever. (Psalms 23:1-6)

I am the Alpha and Omega, the beginning, and the ending... which is, and which was and which to come. (Revelations 1:8)

Nevertheless, not my will, but thine be done. (St. Luke 22:42)

Purge me Lord so that I can be a vessel of honor, sanctified, and meet for the master's use, and prepared unto every good work. (II Timothy 2:21)

Loose the bands of wickedness, undo the heavy burdens, let the oppressed go free, and break every yoke. (Isaiah 58:6)

Cast down imaginations, and every high thing that exalts itself against the knowledge of God and brings into captivity every thought into the obedience of Christ. (II Corinthians 10:5).

Add to my faith virtue, knowledge, temperance, patience, godliness, brotherly kindness, and charity. For if these things be in me, and abound, I will not be barren nor unfruitful. (I Peter 1:5-8)

The fruit of the Spirit is love, joy, peace, longsuffering, gentleness, goodness, faith, meekness, temperance: against such there is no law. (Galatians 5:22-23)

I am fearfully and wonderfully made. (Psalms 139:14)

By the grace of God, I am what I am. (I Corinthians 15:10)

Order my steps in thy word. (Psalms 119:133)

But he was wounded for our transgressions, he was bruised for our iniquities: the chastisement of our peace was upon him; and with his stripes we are healed. (Isaiah 53:5)

Thou wilt keep him in perfect peace whose mind is stayed on thee because he trusts in thee. (Isaiah 26:3)

And the peace of God which passes all understanding, shall keep your hearts and minds through Christ Jesus. (Philippians 4:7)

The joy of the Lord is my strength. (Nehemiah 8:10)

Joy unspeakable and full of glory. (I Peter 1:8)

It is of the Lord's mercies that we are not consumed, because his compassion fails not, they are new every morning, great is thy faithfulness. (Lamentations 3:22-23)

God is not a man, that he should lie; neither the Son of man, that he should repent: hath he said, and shall he not do it? or hath he not spoken, and shall he not make it good? (Numbers 23:19)

That by two immutable things by which it is impossible for God to lie. (Hebrews 6:18)

Jesus Christ is the same yesterday, today and forever. (Hebrews 13:8)

To the only wise God our Savior be glory and majesty, dominion, and glory both now and forever. (Jude 1:25)

And he gave some apostles and some prophets and some evangelists and some pastors and teachers; For the perfecting of the saints, for the work of the ministry, for the edifying of the body of Christ: 'Til we all come into the unity of the faith. (Ephesians 4:11-13)

God is a Spirit and they that worship him must worship him in spirit and in truth. (St. John 4:24)

God is a friend that sticks closer than a brother. (Proverbs 18:24)

God is a Wonderful, Counselor, the mighty God, the everlasting Father, the Prince of Peace. (Isaiah 9:6)

God is the first and the last, and beside him there is no God. (Isaiah 44:6)

God formed man out of the dust of the ground and breathed into his nostrils the breath of life, and man became a living soul. (Genesis 2:7)

God put Adam to sleep and took out one of his ribs and closed the flesh thereof and made a woman and brought her unto the man. (Genesis 2:21-22)

The Word of God is quick and powerful and sharper than any two-edged sword. (Hebrew 4:12)

The Word of God is like a fire and like hammer. (Jeremiah 23:29)

God's Word is so powerful that it will destroy, annihilate, cut to pieces, crush to smithereens, wash away, and put to death everything that is in our lives through our faith in his Word. The Word of God helps us to become a new creation in Christ, old things are passed away, and all things will become new. (II Corinthians 5:17)

Every scripture is written from the King James Version of the Bible.

AUTHOR'S TESTIMONY

I thank God for everything He has done for me; He has completely changed me. He has helped me to make an about face, which is a military term, a 180-degree turn. He has changed my way of thinking and has taught me how to think like He thinks. He has taken out my stony heart and given me a heart of flesh; loving, compassionate, caring for the welfare of others. I am no longer envious or jealous of others. He has calmed my mind and spirit and I am completely free. God is my everything. And He is my source, my all-in-all, He is everything that I need Him to be and so much more. He is with me every step of the way. He has delivered me from my opinions about myself and from the opinions of others. He is continually making me strong in Him and in the power of His might. He has helped me to accomplish things, and He has given me the desires of my heart. I am what I am by the Grace of God. He has taught me how to become independent and to completely trust in Him. My relationship with God is so amazing, He directs my life, He loves me unconditionally, my enemies are at peace with me, I am living my best life. God is Phenomenal!!! What a Gracious, Merciful and Mighty God we serve.

DR. JACKIE KINSLOW

AUTHOR'S BIOGRAPHY

I am including my BIOGRAPHY to DEMONSTRATE TO EACH READER OF THIS BOOK what God can do for anyone who puts their faith, trust, and confidence in Him.

SKILLS

Interpersonal Communication Skills, Empathy, Effective listening, Socialization, Spiritual Support, Time Management, Organization, Patience, Tolerance, Flexibility and Resilience, Hospice Plan Care, Worship Leader, Praise Team, Pastoral Ministry Servant Leadership, Care Ethics, Crisis Intervention, Grief and Bereavement Counseling.

EXPERIENCE

Bible Study and Sunday School Teacher, Preacher, Altar Worker, Praise Team Member March 2018 to Present.

Chaplain/Ordained Minister: Provides direct spiritual support to members/families, including meditation, prayer, counseling, dealing with life threatening illnesses and death. Serve as a mentor/preceptor for new chaplains. Performs spiritual assessments to identify patient/family needs. Assists patient/family with arrangements for funeral or memorial services. Assists with bereavement follow-up services in collaboration with Church Bereavement Coordinator. Prepare and deliver sermons for worship services.

Bible Study/Sunday School Teacher: Conduct weekly regularly scheduled bible study and services. Provide services for those individuals who are unable to attend regularly scheduled services. Develop programs of spiritual care that include spiritual assessment, direct pastoral care, and program evaluation components. Selecting scriptures or materials that will be used therapeutically for assigned populations based on need.

Outreach/Care Ministry: Coordinate special services, health awareness, symposium, and interfaith meetings as called for by population served. Participate in the annual back to school giveaway. Serve as the church campaign fundraiser for annual Thanksgiving food drive with San Manuel Morongo issues, Indian Reservation and Casino where they donate turkeys. Provide support referrals as needed to community organizations and resources. Provide counsel on medical ethical issues, like advance directives, high blood pressure, diabetes, terminal diseases, breast cancer, domestic violence, self-care, self-defense in the context of the religious faith perspective.

Minister's Wife 1979; Pastoral Development, Financial Secretary Praise Leader, Christian Education Teacher, Director of Women's Ministry, Altar Worker, Chaplain,

Bereavement Coordinator, Outreach October 1981 – March 2015

Pastoral Development: Led church in understanding, embracing, and accomplishing mission to develop disciples locally and globally, and engaging followers in worship, community, and assisted in pastoral efforts such as biblical counseling, wedding, and funeral services. Planned worship services and events and equipped staff and lay leaders to coordinate services and events: oversaw staff and ensured they had the resources to fulfill duties and responsibilities. Worked with Outreach Committee to implement ministries reaching out to unchurched, inactive, and new residents of the community, direct assimilation of new members into the congregation. Guided under the direction of the pastor the church in discovery and fulfillment of its calling and mission, including casting God's vision, encouraging spiritual development, leading congregation, and expanding congregation participation in mission activities. Planned and delivered weekly sessions. Strengthened and oversaw faith life by creating inviting community of faith, empowering leadership, coordinating, and supervising weekly staff meetings, and leading weekly gatherings such as bible study. Collaborated with Finance and Stewardship Ministry Group to manage Church's finances and devise strategies to grow stewardship. Provided pastoral care, including hospital, shut-in, bereavement, and funeral visitation, guided and counseled congregation.

Assisted senior pastor to achieve mission objectives, conduct church teaching, and plan weekend services. Led Bible study classes, prayed with church members and guests, and visited with grieving church members. Provides emotional and spiritual intervention in crisis situations. Administered and/or facilitated sacramental, ritual, and devotional experiences. Leads worship services.

Sunday School Teacher: Taught adult, young adult, and beginner's class. Prepared curriculum and handouts for the class. Tabulated School attendance for quarterly church business meetings. Delegated sections of lesson plans to students to co-teach the lesson based on their abilities and expertise.

Church Board Member: Attended quarterly church council meetings to assist in determining church calendar. Preacher/Teacher/Conference & Workshop Speaker. Preached the entire counsel of the Bible. Taught God's principles in faithfulness and sound doctrine.

Sunday School Trophy Committee President and Assistant Secretary, Minister's & Deacon's Wives Secretary and President. South Central District Fellowship Meeting District Elder's Wife March 1984; Minister's & Deacon's Wives President. Suffragan Bishop's Wife November 2014

LICENSES

Chaplain Certificate & Ordination July 2020

Doctor of Philosophy, Church Administration Counseling July 2012

Master of Arts in Theology July 2012

Bachelor of Science in Biblical Studies July 2012

Ordained Pastor's Wife 1986

Ordained Minister 2010

Ordained Minister July 2012

Ordained Minister January 2019

Business Owner: Jaccee's Boutique, a fine Men and Women's Clothing Boutique. "Have suits will travel". June 2002 – June 2017

PERSONAL PUBLICATIONS:

"W.E. W.I.N." Women Empowering Women In Need, 2012,

How To Start A Church or Women's Ministry, 2012

I BROKE THE CURSE

www.ingramcontent.com/pod-product-compliance
Lightning Source LLC
Chambersburg PA
CBHW070049120526
44589CB00034B/1604